Western Locomotives

A Tribute

BERNARD MILLS

KEY
Books

BRITAIN'S RAILWAYS SERIES, VOLUME 7

Front cover image: D1061 *Western Envoy* passing Witham Friary with 1B35, the 10.30 Paddington–Paignton on 17 March 1973.

Back cover image: On 18 March 1975, D1068 *Western Reliance* passes Cheston, near South Brant, where the railway actually runs within the Dartmoor National Park, with 1B45, the 11.30 Paddington–Penzance. Brent Hill makes for a fine backdrop.

Title page image: The era of the Westerns in charge of the West of England expresses is recalled as D1064 *Western Regent* observes the Newton Abbot call with 1A09, the 16.10 Penzance–Paddington, on 20 April 1974. Like so many others we shall experience, this is now a much changed scene.

Published by Key Books
An imprint of Key Publishing Ltd
PO Box 100
Stamford
Lincs PE19 1XQ

www.keypublishing.com

ISBN 978 1 913870 03 4

Typeset by SJmagic DESIGN SERVICES, India.

Contents

Introduction

S oliloquy comes from the Latin word Soliloquium which means talking to oneself. A soliloquy allows the audience, in this case the reader, to know what a person is thinking, and I am thinking of that wonderful class of locomotive that proved to be the final flowering of Great Western Railway (GWR) inherited independence. They were essentially designed by and for the Western Region, which saw hydraulic transmission as the way forward in replacing the beloved Kings, Castles and other 4-6-0 types that Swindon had produced.

The rest of British Rail went down the road of electric transmission but the argument of which was better is a subject way beyond the terms of reference of this tome. As the mistakes of the wholesale lunge into dieselisation came to fruition, BR opted for a standard policy and the Western Region was forced to comply. It was in 1967 that the death warrant for the hydraulics was signed, facts like the versatility of the class to be hauling a fast express from Paddington to Bristol, the South West or into South Wales one day and then the next to be taking china clay down a Cornish branch line or demonstrating their robust abilities on the developing stone traffic from the Mendips counting for nothing.

Under the TOPS system introduced in the early 1970s, the Westerns were assigned Class 52 but were not renumbered like most other stock due to their impending demise. It would take a decade to finally end the hydraulic era and, for me, it was indeed fortunate that in those years I had the means and the opportunity to capture them in action. I did not set out to photograph all 74, indeed I only discovered this had been achieved when sorting out the slides for a valedictory slide show not long after their final demise. I started looking at the various numbers written on the slide mounts and wondered if they were all there and indeed they were, twice over in fact, although I have to admit that with a handful of the more camera-shy members of the class it has been a bit of a struggle.

In this day and age of digital photography, we take quality and high ASA settings for granted. In the Western era, it was a case of trying to make sure the camera was as far as possible able to cope with the films and their speed ratings of the day. By 1965, AGFA 50 ASA had become available, and when I discovered the joys of 64 ASA Ektachrome in 1967, there was the ability to get that critical higher shutter speed and deal with the more challenging lighting conditions, especially when the sun was conspicuous by its absence. Thus I do not present an album full of iconic views such as on the Dawlish–Teignmouth sea wall, topping Dainton and the South Devon Banks, or traversing the Cornish viaducts while all portrayed on nice sunny days through rose-tinted spectacles, but instead offer a varied selection of images taken in all winds and weathers and a good number from well beyond my normal West Country haunts.

There are views of the class, including the common and the rare, in places familiar and not so familiar, while they are on a variety of workings that illustrate their versatility. I have to admit that with some of the more camera-shy members of the class, I am limited in what I can show, hence my apologies if a few pictures do not match the standards we expect nowadays. I found it annoying when I was out photographing, especially in the late 1960s and early 1970s before withdrawals commenced, that my camera kept meeting the same members of the class and in particular those which would survive very much into the closing days of the era, such is life.

Enjoy the pictures, they are a portrait of a railway undergoing great change from steam days; some stations still had goods yards while mechanical signalling still largely characterised the scene. Other

A classic location seen at its best in the winter sunshine as D1055 *Western Advocate* rounds the curve on the approach to Shaldon Bridge, just to the west of Teignmouth, with the Sunday version of the down Cornish Riviera, 1B15, the 10.30 Paddington–Penzance, on 5 January 1975.

than the early Mk.2 stock, the coaches that the Westerns hauled were those which had been pulled by steam as were many of the humble goods wagons that were so much an integral part of the railway. Then there were the van trains, each one with its own motley collection of vehicles, often including stock that pre-dated Nationalisation and not all of GWR origin.

I wish to express my thanks and gratitude to those who have assisted me greatly in the production of this book: Barry Jones for his miracles with modern-day technology; Roger Geech for his help with scanning and information; Martin Street for his assistance particularly in train identification; and Amyas Crump for additional information. I must also thank Jonathon Jackson, Anita Baker and the team at Key Publishing for their belief in me and making this volume possible and congratulate them on the finished product. Then there are the train crews who drove these magnificent machines, the fitters who kept them on the road, and those in charge at Laira Depot, particularly in the final couple of years of the class, who responded in magnificent style to the not infrequent number of requests for a Western to appear on certain trains and diagrams. Take for example the 1976 summer Saturday 09.10 Falmouth–Paddington, which was booked for a Class 50. My requests to ensure a Class 52 appeared on this diagram were duly fulfilled to ensure there were at least half a dozen chances to get those rare locations on the Falmouth Branch in the frame. This book does not set out to be a history of the class; this has been well documented elsewhere. My offering is a pictorial glimpse of what I saw from when I could afford a decent camera in 1965, when the locos were just four years on from their debut, through to their demise just 12 years later.

Unusually for a large class of locomotives, each bore the same prefix which gave them a unique identity. Let your mind drift in thought with me as we take an evocative journey through those words that followed that hallowed prefix, across heraldry, romance, the military and royalty. Names we knew and still love, and each conjuring up its own memories. Enjoy the nostalgia.

D1000 *Western Enterprise*

The pioneer member of the class rests in Platform 4 at Penzance on the seaward side of the train shed on 6 October 1972 after its dash through the night with a train rarely seen by many, 1B85, the 00.35 Paddington–Penzance news. The load of four vehicles certainly aided its rapid nocturnal progress; newspapers were sorted on board by newsagent wholesale staff, who held season tickets endorsed for use on this train. By the time the train came to rest at its destination around 07.30, the West Country had had its newspapers delivered.

A further study of D1000 at Penzance on that same quiet morning, this time looking towards the stop blocks as a lone trader's van goes about its business. The angle clearly shows that the loco's name and number plates were larger than those of the rest of the fleet. This is now a much changed scene as the goods shed and associated buildings were demolished around 1983 to make way for the local tourist information centre and the bus station.

D1001 *Western Pathfinder*

The seasonal 08.10 Kensington Olympia to St Austell Motorail service (1V34), which also served Totnes en route, was always a good bet for a Western to be at the helm, with D1001 seen approaching Par with the down service on 11 May 1974. On this occasion, the service was running about two hours late due a hot axlebox at Taunton. If the left arm of the bracket signal had been pulled off, the points would have been set for taking the Newquay branch. Note to the left the former Pinnock Tunnel signal box (Fowey–St Blazey line), which was deposited here for a while after its closure in January 1958. Although heavily overgrown, the scene remains familiar today.

A scene typical of the early 1970s as D1001 passes Laira Junction with 1A48, the 10.55 Penzance–Paddington, otherwise known as the up 'Cornish Riviera', on 2 May 1971. The former steam shed is to the top left of the picture while the signal box would close and the signals vanish from 10 November 1973 when the Plymouth Panel Box took control of the area. With a Network Rail radio mast in the right foreground and housing now occupying the site of the former Up Sidings in the distance, along with track layout changes and vegetation growth, a much-changed scene exists here today.

D1002 *Western Explorer*

A serene scene as D1002 sweeps round the long curve at Hungerford Common with 1A47, the 10.28 Newquay to Paddington, on 15 August 1970. The train is no doubt full of holidaymakers returning from the delights of the north Cornish coast to the day-to-day trudge of life in the capital. Hungerford station can just be picked out in the background while, to the right, are the peaceful waters of the River Dun, a tributary of the River Kennet.

A rare angle taken from the 'Glamorgan' railtour formed of Class 116 DMU W51138, W59448 and W51151 at Llantrisant as D1002 hurries west with 1C11, the 08.00 Paddington–Fishguard boat train, on 22 July 1972. The special had just returned from Llanharry, at this time the surviving section of the former Cowbridge branch which had been retained for traffic from Llanharry iron ore mine. The last ore train would run three years and three days after this picture was taken and the rails lifted two years later. Doubtless an unrepeatable scene today.

D1003 *Western Pioneer*

The Westerns were not a common sight on the former Southern Railway main line from Waterloo to Exeter. However, on Easter Sunday 1974 (April 14), all Paddington–Plymouth/Penzance trains in each direction were diverted from Castle Cary to Exeter via Yeovil Pen Mill and Honiton, providing some rare photographic opportunities. Well off its normal beaten track, D1003 with 1B33, the 14.30 Paddington to Penzance, does not look out of place in the rural east Devon countryside at Talaton.

There is a fine display of vintage vehicles on show in the car park as D1003 eases off the short 1 in 65 climb up from Brown Queen Tunnel and runs into Bodmin Road – it was not a Parkway then as the name changed from 4 November 1983 – with 1M96, the 11.10 Penzance–Manchester Piccadilly. Seen on 21 July 1973, the train was then one of the very few to traverse the North & West route via Hereford and Shrewsbury.

D1004 *Western Crusader*

A green period piece; D1002, D1003 and D1004, along with D1035 to D1038, were painted in green on their introduction into service as the Western Region had not fully made up its mind what colour the class should carry. The green livery with the small yellow warning panels and red name and number plates is shown to good effect in this low-level view of Laira Junction as the engine makes its way into Plymouth station to work the 16.30 to Paddington on 15 August 1965. The picture of D1001 working the up Cornish Riviera was taken from the Embankment Road bridge in the background.

Looking the other way, a portrait of the changing scene of the mid-1960s shows the railway in transition from steam to diesel. To the left of D1004 is the deserted former Laira steam shed (83D) which closed in October 1964 and now lies abandoned with the rails to the coaling stage already lifted. Behind this stand the roundhouse to the right and the Long or New Shed of 1931 to the left, where the early diesels were based until the purpose-built diesel depot opened in 1961. It all awaits the demolition crew, who would do their worst, starting in December 1966.

D1005 *Western Venturer*

The Western era was not always one of nice clean engines going about their daily business; sadly a not uncommon feature in the latter half of the 1960s was that some locos ran in deplorable external condition. This point is exemplified by a grubby D1005 as it approaches Dawlish Warren with 1A98, the 15.20 Penzance–Paddington, on 7 June 1966. There was nothing wrong with the internals though as *Venturer* would go on to attain a total of 1,392,000 miles in traffic, the highest mileage of the fleet. Note the period camping coaches parked up in their then still rail-connected siding.

Well off the beaten track, Heathfield was rare ground for the class as D1005 runs round its 6Z06 weedkilling train on 11 June 1973, here recorded from the A38 road bridge looking towards Moretonhampstead. At this time, the double-track junction to the former Teign Valley branch was still in place as this was used as a headshunt to reach the goods yard to the right. It is a much changed scene here now with the buildings long gone along with the Teign Valley and the route towards Moretonhampstead, and what is left is heavily overgrown.

D1006 *Western Stalwart*

A very rare capture on film as D1006 was released from a repaint at Laira, on 19 July 1974, without the BR double arrow emblem applied to the cabsides. It ran in this condition for 12 days until the emblems were applied at Laira on the last day of the month. During this short period, I caught up with the engine between Friary Junction and Friary, pure Southern metals I must add, with the empty stock of a 13.20 Paddington–Plymouth relief on 29 July.

The viewpoint is the footbridge just to the west of St Austell station, which was provided to maintain pedestrian access over the tracks when the level crossing at this location was closed on 21 September 1931. In an earlier incarnation, the structure connected the platforms at the former St Blazey station, which closed for normal passenger traffic on 21 September 1925. The autumn colours are starting to show as D1006 slows for the St Austell stop with 1A69, the 08.35 Penzance–Paddington, on 27 October 1973.

D1007 *Western Talisman*

One of the more camera-shy Westerns, D1007 makes its way through the lush fields in Aller Vale, as seen from Barn Owl Bridge, so named after the still going strong and much recommended nearby hostelry. The loco is about to pass Aller Junction with 1A05, the 11.55 Paignton–Paddington, on 28 May 1972. This is a scene that has changed greatly with the opening of the South Devon Link Road on 15 December 2015, the road being known locally as the Kingskerswell by-pass.

The shadows lengthen late in the evening and six days before the summer Solstice on 15 June 1971, as D1007 makes the Newton Abbot call at 20.28 with the down 'Golden Hind', the 17.30 Paddington–Plymouth. This express was a train born of the Western era on 15 June 1964 and aimed at the business market from the South West to give fast access to and from the capital with the ability to do the journey comfortably in a day. The up 07.05 service from Plymouth called only intermediately at Newton Abbot, Exeter and Taunton with a Paddington arrival of 10.55, while the 17.20 (later 17.30) return provided an equally speedy return to these stations. The service was unsurprisingly an instant success.

D1008 *Western Harrier*

D1008 rounds the curve at Aller Junction with 1A71, the 16.30 Plymouth–Paddington, better known as 'The Mayflower' on 30 April 1971. This typical daily scene is one where not very much of it survives. The physical junction between the main and Paignton lines and the signal box were removed in May 1987 when the Exeter Panel signal box took control of the area. Our viewpoint, a farm occupation bridge, was blown up on Christmas Day 2013 to allow its removal as part of the major works in the construction of the South Devon Link Road, the end result being a totally transformed scene with no scope whatsoever for an updated photograph.

A hazy sort of day greets D1008 on 4 May 1974, as it climbs out of the Glynn Valley and up the 1 in 63 gradient, no doubt emitting a suitably wonderful Maybach sound, with 1E21, the Penzance to Bradford Exchange 'Cornishman'. A reminder of the past is the stop board on the down line advising 'All Down Goods and Mineral Trains Must Stop Dead Here', this of course being to pin down wagon brakes for the descent to Lostwithiel in the era before fully fitted freight trains.

D1009 *Western Invader*

Memories of summer Saturdays in the west are rekindled as D1009 drops down the 1 in 71 gradient from Churston at Waterside with 1E48, the 08.52 Kingswear–Leeds, while the returning holidaymakers enjoy their final views of Torbay on 23 August 1969. Not a lot has changed here; the Paignton–Kingswear section survives as part of the Dartmouth Steam Railway and a now larger and modern Waterside Caravan Park behind the train is still doing good business. Little did I know at the time that I would spend much of the summer of 1984 courting the future Mrs Mills in this delightful cove.

D1009 passes Thornford Bridge Halt, to the south of Yeovil Pen Mill, with the summer Saturday 06.50 Derby–Weymouth (1O53) on 14 August 1976. The line here had been singled from 26 May 1968, while this service and its corresponding 13.20 return were the only (and last) expresses booked to run over the erstwhile GWR route to the South Coast resort. My request to the authorities at Laira to have words with their friends at Bath Road to provide suitable motive power for the train from Bristol on this day paid dividends!

D1010 *Western Campaigner*

Two for the price of one with a rarely photographed location and a flash back to when all was maroon. I am riding behind D1010 on 1N21, the 11.10 Penzance–Bradford, on 29 August 1965, as the train takes the crossover at Rattery due to single line working from Brent on the down line for Sunday engineering work. Waiting its onward passage is D1040 *Western Queen*, which was about 40 minutes late with 1C45, the 09.30 Paddington to Plymouth. Rattery Siding signal box closed on 11 August 1972, and no trace of it remains. Single line working for engineering possessions is taboo on the privatised railway of today; passengers are herded onto the dreaded rail replacement buses instead.

Who will forget the rare and unlikely sight of D1010 at Treherbert at the head of the Rhondda Fawr with Pen-Pych, or Table Mountain, for a back drop, which is unique in being the only three-sided flat-topped mountain in the world. The loco is running round its stock off 1Z20, the 08.20 Paddington–Treherbert 'Western Requiem' railtour, on 13 February 1977. The world and his wife wander freely observing the proceedings with not an orange or yellow jacket to be seen. This is a greatly changed scene today due to a combination of vegetation growth, track removal and substantial landscaping work being undertaken, with the bank to the left now no more.

D1011 *Western Thunderer*

Fondly known by some as 'Thunder box', a more humble duty on the South Wales main line was the order of the day as D1011 makes the call at Patchway with the 17.45 Cardiff Central–Bristol Temple Meads local service on 21 August 1974. Although a number of people alighted from the train, there was only one joining passenger, your photographer! I suspect the returning commuters in their train of seven Mk.1 carriages would have had a more pleasant journey than their present-day counterparts crammed into an inadequate Sprinter unit.

The rhododendrons are in full bloom as D1011 is about to enter Marley Tunnel on 1 July 1972, with the well-loaded 16.00 St Austell to Kensington Olympia (1M01) Motorail service. The up line here makes a small divergence as the tunnel is actually two separate single line bores side by side – D1011 will pass through the later of the two – dating from 14 May 1893 when the line was doubled from Rattery to Brent. From a point just to the west of Ivybridge, the main line actually runs through the Dartmoor National Park until leaving it on exiting the tunnel.

D1012 *Western Firebrand*

I do find it hard to imagine that Newton Abbot did once look like this. Gone are the signal boxes, the signals and the greater majority of the track work; for example, the up main to the left with the up through alongside are now a car park. To the right, the former motive power depot and the carriage sidings with their long welded rails are now an industrial estate, the carriage works to the immediate right is now a supermarket and the power station, which oversaw the scene, was demolished in the spring of 1975. D1012 heads west at 17.49 with 1C60, the 14.30 Paddington to Penzance, on 28 April 1971.

It is a crisp autumn day on 26 October 1973, as D1012 is captured running alongside what was then the abandoned Kennett & Avon canal between the former Wolfhall Junction and Crofton. The train is the lengthy 11.00 Fridays-only Plymouth–Paddington, often loading to 13 or 14 coaches, and returning as the 16.53 Paddington to Penzance. I can happily report a changed scene here for the better with the canal fully restored and full of water and boats. On the rails, perhaps not such good news as lengthy trains for weekend and other peaks do not have a place on the railway of the 21st century.

D1013 *Western Ranger*

It is to a route where not that many pictures of the class are to be found, namely the North & West, otherwise known as the Welsh Marches. D1013, hauling 1Z18, the 09.40 Paddington–Hereford railtour, makes a fine sight climbing the 1 in 95 grade at Llanvihangel Crucorney with the southern edge of the Brecon Beacons for a hazy backdrop. Running on 26 September 1976, this train was also captured leaving Box Tunnel and then pursued in my little 100E car; we made it to Llanvihangel with about 30 seconds to spare, the things we did in our youth!

D1013 is seen on railtour duty again on 25 October 1975, this time to the more far flung parts of West Wales as the 'Pembroke Coast Express' run by the Wirral Railway Circle makes a photographic stop at Whitland. The 1950s architecture is clearly on show to the left on the down platform, when the station saw the effects of the Modernisation Plan. This was a memorable trip with D1013 taking us to Fishguard, Milford Haven and Pembroke Dock. I had only retuned the previous week from a six-month secondment to Brit Rail Travel International in New York; what a superb way to renew my acquaintance with the Class 52s!

D1014 *Western Leviathan*

D1014 calls at a rundown Churston with the summer Saturday 14.35 Kingswear–Paddington (1A67) at a time when the Paignton to Kingswear line was run as a basic railway. By this date, 26 July 1969, the crossing loop and all signalling had been removed and the former Brixham branch had been lifted, hence the empty bay platform. Note the ancient bus which connected with the nearby holiday camps. It is a transformed scene here now with the station again a crossing place, although this angle is obscured by the workshops of the Dartmouth Steam Railway.

About to enter the short Redruth Tunnel, D1014 passes Drump Lane on 11 May 1974, with 1B45, the 11.30 Paddington–Penzance, with the train formed of a neat rake of Mk.2a stock. Behind the coaches is the former substantial Drump Lane goods shed, while on the opposite side of the track at the rear of the train is the former Drump Lane signal box. Both structures are no more, rendering this a much changed scene.

D1015 *Western Champion*

Of the 80 miles between Plymouth and Penzance, 3¾ miles of it are carried on viaducts, giving rise to classic scenes. Crossing Coombe St Stephen's Viaduct, a couple of miles or so west of Burngullow, is D1015 with the 10.00 Ponsandane–Par empty stock move (5B72) on 28 July 1976. This train came down as the 23.35 Fridays-only Paddington–Penzance, a 12-coach summer relief to the normal overnight train. The stock was then worked to Par, as seen here, to form the 12.15 to Newquay and subsequent 13.23 Newquay–Paddington.

Overleaf: Three weekends after the above picture, I caught up with D1015 again at a classic location that bears the stamp of Brunel's Great Way West. On 22 August, the loco emerges from Box Tunnel with 1Z35, the 08.30 Paddington–Paignton. The western portal of the tunnel was certainly built to impress and shows the greatness of the Great Western.

D1016 *Western Gladiator*

Affectionately known as 'Gladys' to the enthusiasts of the day, D1016 emerges from the short 125-yard Devonport Tunnel on 23 September 1969, and is about to pass through Devonport Albert Road station with 7C56, the 14.55 St Blazey–Tavistock Junction goods. This is a unique tunnel as it actually has another passing directly beneath it in the form of Ford Tunnel on the former Southern Railway route into Plymouth, disused since September 1964. There is only four feet between the crown of the SR tunnel and the rails of the GWR one above.

We have already visited Barn Owl Bridge to see D1007 coming in the opposite direction; this is the view looking towards Newton Abbot as D1016 ambles through Aller Vale with 1B23, the 11.30 Paddington–Paignton, on 22 September 1974. This quiet pastoral scene has since been transformed as the train would now be passing beneath the concrete bridge built to take the road to Kingskerswell from the South Devon Link Road.

D1017 *Western Warrior*

D1017 to D1020 were the only four members of the class not to be air brake fitted, which did restrict their movements as air braked stock came more into use, making them early candidates for withdrawal. D1017 passes over the junction with the former GWR Marlborough branch with 1A35, the 09.40 Plymouth–Paddington, while approaching the remains of Savernake Low Level station on 6 June 1970. This closed with the branch on 9 September 1961, while freight to Marlborough lasted until 7 July 1964; a stub of the branch remaining as a siding at this time.

What goes up must come back; D1017 returned from Paddington with the 16.30 Paddington to Plymouth (1C65), seen here passing through Bedwyn, which was the limit of local services from Reading and Newbury. To the right, behind the little wooden waiting shed, which remarkably still survives, are the placid waters of the River Dun with the adjacent Kennet & Avon canal clearly visible. Despite a few changes such as the bay platform now being a car park, it is still possible to take a decent picture from the road bridge here.

D1018 *Western Buccaneer*

Parallel Westerns! The spotters are gathered as they always did at the west end of Bristol Temple Meads as this gave a grandstand view of Bath Road shed as well as the comings and goings through the station. On 19 May 1973, D1018 runs in on the right with the stock for a 1Z12 special working while, to the left, the train I am about to catch, the 09.30 to Paddington, arrives behind D1052 *Western Viceroy*. There is not a lot of interest or variety for the spotters to see at Temple Meads these days.

The lengthy nameplate of D1018 is clearly visible as the engine brings 1C55, the 12.30 Paddington–Penzance, from England into Cornwall and off the Royal Albert Bridge at Saltash on 9 October 1969. I learnt my trade as a railway clerk at Saltash under the guidance of the late Jim Lewis; this was the view from outside the booking office door, not a bad place to work with things like this going past regularly!

D1019 *Western Challenger*

It is but half a mile west from Saltash to Wearde as D1019 approaches with 1M95, the 08.45 Newquay–Manchester Piccadilly on 29 July 1972, it passing to the left of the former down loop from Saltash. This was taken out of use on 31 October 1965, the same day as the signal box here, which was sited about two-thirds of the way along the length of the train where the March 1908 deviation of the main line begins. There is still a summer Saturday Newquay–Manchester train but this does not leave until 15.20, the five-coach Voyager being totally inadequate for the traffic on offer.

The first picture I ever took at the classic location of Cockwood Harbour. It is high tide on 1 May 1969, as D1019 makes its way over the causeway with 1A79, the 15.05 Penzance to Paddington. Knowledge of the tide tables is a useful asset for this location, which lost some of its character when, towards the end of 2007, Network Rail erected a lineside fence over the causeway. Since then, some bushes have sprouted up but it still remains a popular and reasonable spot for photography, sadly these days not one with many locomotive-hauled trains.

D1020 *Western Hero*

Take no notice of the headcode; this is not the down 'Cornishman' but the afternoon ballast from Meldon Quarry as D1020 hurries through Bow (which would close to passengers three weeks later) on the way to Exeter Riverside on 16 May 1972. The line had been singled from Crediton to Okehampton on 17 October 1971, with redundant track panels dumped on the up platform for the scrap man to collect. The railway line through here is now part of the Dartmoor Railway but, at the time of writing, it faces a very uncertain future.

"Western Hero, Western Queen, that's why Laira keeps them clean. My Lords, My Lords, My Lords." A chant recited by many in the final era of the class on those dwindling service trains they worked and the railtours. I suspect a fair number will take a trip down memory lane and recite these words again and recall a host of memories. A respectable D1020 approaches Saltash with 1E21, the 09.50 Penzance–Bradford Exchange, on 2 October 1969. Note the green Western National buses parked on Culver Road, the bridge over the main line.

D1021 *Western Cavalier*

Returning to former Southern Metals in the West Country, another picture from the Easter Sunday diversions of 14 April 1974, and a rare location for one of these as D1021 has just emerged from the 1,345-yard Honiton Tunnel (the longest in Devon) with 1B29, the 12.30 Paddington–Plymouth. This view is now both inaccessible and overgrown, with anything other than a Class 159 being a novelty.

A rare angle for D1021 with the lengthy 7B33 (when setting the headcode, the driver could seemingly not count properly) 14.00 Exeter Riverside–Truro goods passing beneath the Normandy Way overbridge, this being taken from Royal Albert Bridge signal box on 22 June 1973, two weeks before it closed. From 2 July, the Plymouth Panel signal box took over the area and the line from here to St Budeaux was singled at the same time, retaining the former up line. So, within a fortnight, the rails upon which we see the loco would carry trains no more.

D1022 *Western Sentinel*

Two for the price of one, to the devotees of hydraulic motive power this was 'double stamps'. D1022 and D1010 provide super-power for a train that will forever remain in the hearts of many, 1M74, the 14.00 Penzance to Birmingham New Street, although on this date, 29 May 1974, another wrong reporting number was being displayed. There was no operational reason for this train to be lavished with such motive power; it was just a convenient way of working a spare engine from Penzance back to Laira Depot. Various combinations of motive power appeared but this was the ultimate.

In the heart of the mining district of west Cornwall, D1022 is about to pass over the level crossing at Dolcoath Siding, between Redruth and Camborne, with a lengthy collection of vans forming 4B05, the 12.50 Penzance–Bristol Temple Meads, on 27 October 1973. *Sentinel* was a popular engine amongst the enthusiasts of the day, gaining the nickname 'Ducks'. I have no idea how this came about, but it was certainly a good workhorse.

D1023 *Western Fusilier*

Memories are recalled of when, in their early days, the class worked to Chester (spring 1962–64) on the Paddington–Birkenhead trains as D1023 heads west out of the city on 29 January 1977. It is crossing the Dee Viaduct by Roodee Racecourse, the oldest in the world, with the 15.30 Crewe–Paddington (1Z08) 'Western Memorial' tour in the last rays of a glorious winter's day. I think the camera and film did very well, the exposure of 125th of a second at F2.8 being taken at 16.21.

D1023 was the last Western to haul a normal service train. A piece of history is made on 23 February 1977, as the loco pulls away in the fading light from Okehampton with 6O99, the 18.30 Meldon Quarry–Salisbury ballast, which was running 90 minutes early with *Fusilier* working it as far as Exeter Riverside. At 17.20 in February, the camera and film have again done well at 125th at F3.5. The crew kindly held the train here for the photographic party from Meldon to catch up again; it cost us a couple of pints but it was a privilege to photograph the last Western in regular service.

D1024 *Western Huntsman*

This was a rather camera-shy machine, but D1024 was captured atop the 13.30 Paddington–Penzance (1B65) on 19 August 1972, as it passed in old money the down Hemerdon distant, the colour light signal towards the rear of the train. The location, which after some fairly recent cutting back by Network Rail is now again clear for photographic purposes, is Backamoor Bridge by Lower Venton Farm. The hills where the rural South Hams meet Dartmoor make for a superb backdrop.

D1024 is nicely parked up in Alstone Sidings at Cheltenham and ready to work 1A49, the 17.00 Cheltenham Spa–Paddington, on 12 September 1971, with the picture taken from behind D28 on 1V83, the 11.00 Sunday service from Liverpool Lime Street to Plymouth. I was returning from my one and only visit to the Irish Republic for a steam tour from Dublin and this was a nice bonus on the way home. It would of course be impossible today to lean out of the carriage window, especially for any impromptu photography.

D1025 *Western Guardsman*

'Western Guards Van' as some called it, D1025 is working hard past the Rhododendrons on the 1 in 67 climb from St Erth towards Penzance with 8Z77, the 06.30 Tavistock Junction to Ponsandane engineers special, on 8 June 1974. I had made my way to the bridge by the St Erth up distant signal for the down 'Cornishman', only to get 50003 in the frame. However, the unexpected appearance of D1025 on this train, which I later learnt had spent a lot of time occupying most of the down loops in Cornwall, was a worthy bonus.

Lovely evening light as the shadows lengthen for D1025 running into the through road at Plymouth station with the Thursdays-only 18.35 Burngullow–Sittingbourne clay slurry (6O42) for the Bowaters paper mill, this being a heavy train that would have required assistance over the South Devon Banks. Photography of this service was somewhat limited as it only ran once a week and by the time it was around the Plymouth area, it was only possible when the days were at their longest, as on this occasion, 11 July 1974. This is another train that sadly now no longer runs.

D1026 *Western Centurion*

D1026 arrives at London Paddington atop 1A05, the 11.55 Paignton–Paddington, with the formation featuring a mixture of Mk.1 and early Mk.2 stock. Of particular interest are the leading two vehicles, these being examples of the experimental XP64 stock that pioneered the introduction of the Mk.2 fleet. I had actually gone up to London on this day, 4 May 1973, to ride on the very last Bristol Pullman, making use of some time to watch the comings and goings at Paddington, which was much more enjoyable then. This is a much changed scene today, especially with the overhead electric wires.

D1026 and a fine rake of Mk.1 stock forming 1V71, the 07.36 Leeds–Penzance, pass the former Devonport Junction, just to the west of Plymouth station, on 11 June 1974. To the right is the course of the former Southern double track main line to Exeter via Okehampton. The section from here to Devonport Kings Road survived for freight until 7 March 1971, the track being lifted about three months later. Nature had already re-claimed the former SR track bed with a display of summer flowers. Stand in the same spot today and one will only see a jungle.

D1027 *Western Lancer*

Just to the east of Plymouth station, D1027 heads 1A19, the 08.30 Sundays-only Plymouth–Paddington, at Mutley on 19 May 1974, as seen from the then new multi-storey car park built over the tracks. The imposing red building behind is the Royal Eye Infirmary. The loco made headline news on 8 April 1964, by setting a new record of running non-stop from Paddington to Plymouth in 208 minutes. A couple of days later, I noted D1027 on the three-coach 11.46 Plymouth–Waterloo, this calling at all stations to Exeter Central and taking the better part of 2½ hours; how the mighty fall!

The glory days of summer Saturdays on the Newquay branch as D1027 breasts Tregoss Summit, the highest point of the line at 515 feet above sea level, with 1A15, the 10.30 Newquay–Paddington, on 24 August 1974. At the time, the bridge took the railway over the A30 road; this was diverted as a dual carriageway slightly to the north in 2007. Reminding us this is china clay country, dominating the skyline behind the train is Wheal Remfrey. This view is now very overgrown and has a much changed backdrop with the Wheal Remfrey sand hills removed.

D1028 *Western Hussar*

Home with the milk as D1028 crosses Coombe-by-Saltash Viaduct and slows for the Saltash stop on 5 August 1976, atop 6A21, the 16.40 St Erth–Acton, with the estuary of the River Tamar just visible behind the train. D1028 was one of the five members of the class fitted with the experimental air grille to improve cab ventilation. The milk was a valuable source of traffic to the railway at £300 per tank, but this finished in August 1979 when the Milk Marketing Board was able to source its needs for London from the Home Counties.

With the air grille clearly visible, D1028 rolls into Exeter St Davids early one morning with 1A25, the 06.40 Newton Abbot to Paddington. Taken on 25 August 1971, not much in this view had changed since steam days with the substantial water tower to the right, proper signals and Exeter West signal box alongside the 1 in 37 grade up to Exeter Central. It all looks a bit different here now but the signal box still survives, although you have to venture to the Crewe Heritage Centre to pay it a visit.

D1029 *Western Legionnaire*

D1029 passes through the remains of the first Ivybridge station, which closed on 2 March 1959 and was demolished in the spring of 1964, with 1B45, the 11.30 Paddington–Penzance, on 3 August 1974. At this time, a siding remained for china clay traffic from the Lee Moor area to the Potteries. The present station opened on 15 July 1994 and is about ½ mile to the east. *Legionnaire* has a pedigree that is often overlooked as it was the last main line locomotive to be built at Swindon Works but it would only be in traffic for just over a decade.

Overleaf: Classic train, classic location: Three Arch Bridge at Follaton, just to the west of Totnes, sees D1029 hard at work lifting the 11-coach 09.15 Liverpool Lime Street to Penzance (1V76) up the 1 in 47 climb of Rattery Bank on 15 April 1974. This was a train of long standing and always a busy one. Since 2010, when cross-country services were recast at the behest of the interfering Department for Transport, direct trains between Merseyside and the South West became no more. Passengers now have to do battle changing at Birmingham New Street.

D1030 *Western Musketeer*

D1030 in the early blue livery with small yellow panels waits in Saltash station on 21 June 1969 to reverse into the yard to collect some milk tanks, which would be attached to the 13.40 from St Erth at Plymouth. It is now a changed scene here with the footbridge having been removed on 9 April 1989, while the down platform only has a bus-type shelter, although the station buildings to the right are now undergoing restoration. The Baptist Church was burnt down on Christmas Day 1987 and replaced by a new building, which opened in March 1992, but any view of it is blocked by vegetation.

A picture not of the best quality but one which is so rare that it stands on its own merits. D1030 is seen passing through the former Brent station on 21 July 1970, with the 4A64 Par to Park Royal Freightliner working. This was a short-lived service and was normally a solid Class 47 diagram; it was running late on this gloomy summer evening, but the number of times a Class 52 Western worked this train can be counted on the fingers of one hand. Brent was once the junction for Kingsbridge and closed on 5 October 1964.

D1031 *Western Rifleman*

Talking of Par, here is D1031 running in to the down platform with the summer Saturday 10.56 Paddington–Penzance (1B39) on 11 May 1974. I suspect a fair contingent of the passengers will change for the waiting DMU to Newquay. For once, I can report this is a scene that looks broadly similar today, albeit with a good measure of background growth, and the Royal Hotel outside the station is still going strong.

Overleaf: There was nothing like a Western in full flight and here is D1031 in such a mode as it rushes past one of my favourite local spots for an afternoon out at Harford, just to the east of Ivybridge, on 13 May 1974. In tow is 1A45, the 12.40 Penzance–Paddington, which was always very identifiable as it had a GUV parcels van marshalled next to the engine. The second Ivybridge station opened in July 1994 and was constructed just to the other side of the road bridge in the background. There is little point in going here now for photography as it is too overgrown.

D1032 *Western Marksman*

For rarity this stands alongside D1030 at Brent on the Freightliner as D1032 hauls a Blue Pullman set, formed of 60091, 60731, 60741, 60740, 60730 and 60090, as 1Z03, the 11.55 Plymouth to Kensington Olympia return 'Holiday Inn Christmas Special'. Recorded on 28 December 1970, the unusual combination is approaching St Mary's Bridge, Plympton, in the snow. The operating authorities did not trust the Blue Pullman sets over the South Devon Banks on their own, so D1032 was provided as an insurance policy. I did not venture out much in such conditions as God did not design my body for cold weather.

D1032 was making a superb sound, I seem to remember, on a heavily laden engineering train at Laira on 23 September 1972. This was actually an open day at the depot and for the assembled multitude, this was an unexpected bonus. Barely four months after this scene was recorded, D1032 had the unfortunate distinction of being the first member of the class to be withdrawn from service.

D1033 *Western Trooper*

The Westerns proved ideal for the heavy stone trains from the Mendips and there was hope that some members of the class might be retained for this traffic, but it was not to be. D1033 is seen passing between the former Grafton East Junction, the embankment of which is to the left towards the rear of the train, and the former Wolfhall Junction, which is just behind the photographer, on 26 October 1973, with the heavily laden 8M53, the 11.10 Westbury–Bletchley. A decent picture can still be taken here, albeit with more foliage and no sign of the aforementioned embankment.

D1033 is in fine fettle as it opens up after a signal check approaching the level crossing at Long Rock while in charge of 1B81, the 08.00 Bristol Temple Meads–Penzance, on 31 July 1972, with the train in earshot of completing its journey. It is a small world as my sister-in-law is now resident in the flat to the left of the engine, which has a lovely balcony to sit on opposite St Michael's Mount and watch the trains go by. The line was singled on 23 June 1974, and there is now little of interest to observe passing by on the rails.

D1034 *Western Dragoon*

It is high summer when, in the week of the longest day, the sun is far enough around to capture the scene on the northern side of Sparkwell Bridge, and one can only imagine the sound as D1034 tops the summit at Hemerdon with 6A21, the 16.40 St Erth–Acton milk. Such was the power of the Westerns, there was no need for assistance over the South Devon Banks, even with a load of just over 20 milk tanks containing between them something just short of 50,000 gallons of milk. The train glistens in the evening sunshine on 18 June 1974.

From the light of summer to that of winter as D1034 basks in the late afternoon low sunshine in Platform 5 at Plymouth on 31 January 1975, having just been attached to work forward into Cornwall with 1V76, the 09.20 Liverpool–Penzance. Other observations noted on that late shift were D1033 with the 14.40 Penzance–Paddington (1A79), D1058 on the 6A19 milk tanks, D1052 with empty stock, D1021 heading 2B24, the 17.30 stopper to Penzance, D1059 with 4B10, the 15.53 Bristol Temple Meads parcels, and D1043 in charge of 1B05, the 16.53 Paddington–Penzance. Going to work then was a pleasure!

D1035 *Western Yeoman*

Me and my shadow! It is that time of the year again when the evening shadows lengthen and the colours mellow. D1035 fits in nicely between the trees as it speeds along the Exe estuary on the approach to Cockwood Harbour with 1C65, the 16.30 Paddington–Penzance, on 1 May 1969. Note the small yellow destination boards placed under the windows on the coaches, a fairly recent innovation of the time designed to make it easier for passengers to identify their trains as opposed to the previous lengthy and wooden roof boards.

Cut and run! D1035 enters Newbury at 19.20 with 1C72, the 18.30 Paddington to Plymouth, on 6 June 1970. It was then a case of a quick dash down the platform and over the footbridge in order to catch the train home to Plymouth; I had pre-arranged the move with the station staff just in case anybody got in the way! My journey was a pleasant one sat in the front compartment listening to D1035 all the way, complete with a few cans of beer to wash down the fish and chips that had been finished not long before pressing the shutter. This was the way to travel.

D1036 *Western Emperor*

The class was indeed maids of all work with D1036 seen in charge of a neat rake of clay hoods from Fowey Docks (Carne Point) to St Blazey on 28 July 1976. This was recorded running beside the estuary of the River Fowey, which was almost at its tidal limit, and fortunately nature was playing ball with a high tide, as seen from Coulsons Park approaching the junction with the main line at Lostwithiel. The long hot summer of '76 was indeed memorable, especially for the lack of wind that enabled reflections like this to be captured.

From the warmth of summer to a cold and frosty spring morning as D1036 runs round 1Z58, the 07.15 from Plymouth 'Western Sunset' railtour, prior to the 09.05 departure from Exeter St Davids, on 29 March 1975. This was then routed via the former London and South Western main line to Yeovil Junction and thence to Westbury, where D1052 took over for the onward run to Derby. This engine was instantly recognisable as it was the only member of the class to have its number plates set higher than the nameplates, and this feature shows up clearly in this image.

D1037 *Western Empress*

We have met the emperor at Exeter St Davids, so move along the platform to greet its wife. D1035–D1038 were the only members of the Crewe-built Westerns to carry green livery. D1037 has come off 1A28, the 06.00 from Penzance, on the adjoining Platform 5 to pick up 2C26, the 08.23 from Kingswear portion that was waiting in Platform 6, before setting off at 09.55 for Paddington on 18 August 1966. It is a different scene here now as the buildings behind the engine have been demolished to make way for a new traincare depot.

Overleaf: The hydraulic era at its zenith is recorded in the classic view from the Bath Road Depot balcony as D1037 sets off from Bristol Temple Meads, having taken over 1V73, the 08.50 Liverpool Lime Street–Plymouth, which at this time would have come from Crewe via Shrewsbury and Hereford. Also on show in hydraulic heaven on 25 August 1969 were Hymek D7005 waiting to leave Bath Road while stabled to the right is D1021 with D1032 and D868 above while an unidentified Hymek waits to come on shed. This view point, I am sorry to report, is no more.

D1038 *Western Sovereign*

D1038 on 1A65, the 08.35 Penzance–Paddington, exits Weston Mill Viaduct and passes the junction with the line into Devonport Dockyard on the approach to Keyham on 22 March 1973. The fine double arm bracket signal would fall victim to the Plymouth Panel extension just four months later, while the viewpoint and the footbath over the viaduct would be sealed off early in 2008 due to security concerns with the naval base. The background is now dominated by the unsightly incinerator commissioned in the spring of 2015.

The hydraulic era at Shrewsbury was short-lived, lasting only two years from early 1962, with the odd blip in 1967–68, so it is little wonder that enthusiasts are getting excited as they no doubt cop what would have been a rare visitor here by this time. On 12 May 1973, D1038 arrives at Shrewsbury with 1Z54, the 06.35 Plymouth to Aberystwyth excursion. Some very co-operative staff at Laira arranged for the train to be Western-hauled to and from Shrewsbury, and I was allowed a premature exit to run forward and record the scene!

D1039 *Western King*

This was a very camera-shy member of the class and one of the early withdrawals. Having emerged from Whiteball Tunnel from Somerset into Devon, D1039 on 1C65, the 16.30 Paddington to Penzance, breasts the summit at Whiteball in the evening colours at the start of the descent towards Tiverton Junction on 29 August 1970.

One of those annoying moments endured more often than not in railway photography, full sun as the train approaches until the unwanted arrival of a rogue cloud which covers the scene at the precise moment the train is in the frame, and full sun again as the last coach passes by. Such was the case for D1039 approaching Shaldon Bridge, just to the west of Teignmouth, on 29 March 1972, with 1M23, the 10.55 Plymouth–Manchester Piccadilly. With such a rare engine, one just has to take it on the chin and apologise for the quality of the picture.

D1040 *Western Queen*

A king must have a consort, so here is its queen, just over four miles up the line. Not a picture taken under the lockdown conditions during which I write these words, but the Dawlish sea wall looking at its best in the glow of morning winter sunshine before the world has really woken up. The view is from Langstone Rock as D1040, hauling 1Z25, the 09.20 Plymouth–Paddington relief, leaves the seaside behind and takes the curve around to Dawlish Warren on 5 January 1975.

Despite their rundown, the Westerns were often to be seen on the Paddington to Birmingham services, where they gave some excellent performances, until surprisingly late in their careers. Such memories are recalled as coming out of the morning mist, D1040 is seen at Lapworth on 1M11, the 09.05 Paddington–Birmingham New Street, on 7 February 1975. The evidence of the short-sighted rationalisation of the former quadruple track here is sadly only too evident.

D1041 *Western Prince*

The sun has just pierced through the early-morning sea mist to beautifully illuminate D1041 and its train ready to depart Falmouth (the 'Docks' suffix was not added until 15 May 1989) with the 09.10 Falmouth–Paddington (1A79) on 18 September 1976. After an absence of a few years, Falmouth gained a through summer Saturday service, mainly to ease congestion at Long Rock. The train was booked for a Class 50 but some words were exchanged with the kind people at Laira Depot for a variation on some days; need I say more?

The requirement not to show the train headcode had been introduced by BR early in 1976, so instead the headcode display was often wound to show the locomotive number or, in this case, some of it. *Prince* nearly made it to the end, being withdrawn in the final week of operation of the class, and won the hearts of many by just keeping going when not in the best external condition, having last visited Swindon Works in April 1970. On 3 July 1976, D1041 is seen at Exeter West with 1B73, the 14.30 Paddington–Paignton, as it passes a splendid array of signals.

D1042 *Western Princess*

This was another class member that did not like having its picture taken. The lush South Devon countryside is at its best as D1042 *Western Princess* passes Dinnaton to the west of Ivybridge in charge of 1C55, the 12.30 Paddington–Penzance, on 8 June 1970. After many years of growth, this location was severely cut back by Network Rail in the spring of 2018; the view is actually even clearer of vegetation than when I took this picture.

It is a dull evening in west Cornwall as D1042 rolls into Camborne with 1C55, the 12.30 Paddington–Penzance, on 18 August 1969. The loco is passing over the level crossing that still manages to bring the traffic in the town to a grinding halt at times. Of particular interest is the rather insecure-looking centre arm balance signal, complete with lower arm distant for Roskear Junction (seven chains to the east), clinging on for dear life to the side of the footbridge.

D1043 *Western Duke*

Staying in the heart of the west Cornwall mining district, it is just over a mile up the line from Roskear Junction to the site of Carn Brea station, which closed on 2 January 1961. Just approaching the location is D1043 on 8 July 1974, with 2B24, the 17.42 Plymouth–Penzance stopping service. The load on this train was unpredictable, ranging from two coaches to 14 if Plymouth Argyle were playing at home and, if the latter were doing well, a relief to this train was not unknown.

Sadly, much of the changing scene of the 1970s was that of closed railway lines, abandoned stations, lifted tracks and redundant signals. Such is the case here as D1043 leans on the curve into the former Brent station atop 1B45, the 11.30 Paddington–Penzance, on 20 July 1974. To the right of the train is the site of the junction with the former Kingsbridge branch, which closed on 9 September 1963. The once proud bracket signal is now devoid of its arms, having been made redundant on the extension of the Plymouth Panel signal box from 17 December 1973.

D1044 *Western Duchess*

A duke must have a duchess; here is D1044 passing Bethany, between Menheniot and St Germans, on 7 March 1974, with a lengthy and impressive collection of assorted vans forming 4M05, the 12.50 Penzance to Crewe. Conveying perishable traffic, the train ensured that the produce of the west reached the markets of the north in time for their early opening. Varying on the season and the nature of the traffic, I have known this train to stand in Saltash station for 20 minutes to be loaded.

The impressive train shed over platforms 1 to 3 at Penzance station shows up well as D1044, having been shunt released from its inward working, makes its way out of the station on 20 May 1972, prior to berthing in the sea wall siding, where the engine would await the call to return to Plymouth. Note the conveniently timed Western National bus to the right, making its way along Chyandour Cliff, a curious name for a road.

D1045 *Western Viscount*

Our journey through the nobility continues with a picture that marked a milestone for me, the first one taken on my new camera when I could afford to upgrade to a Praktica Nova camera with Tessar lens. A good choice of subject to christen the new equipment, D1045 on 1C45 makes its way off the Royal Albert Bridge into Saltash station with the down 'Cornish Riviera', the 10.30 Paddington–Penzance, on 9 October 1969. Notice the lack of traffic on the then eight-year-old Tamar Road Bridge.

An attractive scene as D1045 rounds the curve at Livermead and crosses the Cockington Road bridge, about half a mile to the west of Torquay, with 1B55, the 12.30 Paddington–Paignton. The Western does not have far to go to reach the journey's end on 19 April 1974, while the formation is a mix of Mk.1 and Mk.2 stock, which was very common in this period.

D1046 *Western Marquis*

Although the Paddington to Penance main line is the way to the west, for the first ten miles of its course from Exeter, the rails actually head south before making the turn to go in the right direction upon reaching the coast at Dawlish Warren. The flat and level stretch across the fields and marshes towards Exminster has always been known as the race track and on this stretch of line, D1046 is in a hurry with 1A75, the 14.40 Penzance–Paddington, on 10 June 1972, as it powers past the Exminster up advanced starting signal.

D1046 was in a rush once again when photographed running at speed with 1B45, the 11.30 Paddington–Penzance, on what was then the quadruple track section from Cogload Junction (the signal box of which can just be glimpsed to the left of the rear of the train) to Taunton. Seen on 4 January 1975, this pleasant scene in Taunton Deane is not quite the same now as, in the immediate right foreground, there now stands a rather bland Network Rail relay room enclosed within an equally ugly metal fence, and vegetation growth mars the view of those green fields.

D1047 *Western Lord*

One of those days when the sun is playing mostly in rather than out, the weather gods oblige with a lovely cloud formation behind D1047, this looking superb in the pale blue livery with small yellow warning panels. The loco is rounding the curve at Sparkwell, on the approach to Hemerdon Siding, at speed with 1C55, the 12.30 Paddington to Penzance, on 6 March 1970.

The view from Kit Hill Crescent in the western suburbs of Plymouth as D1047 with 4M05, the 12.50 Penzance–Crewe, descends the 1 in 79 grade from the Royal Albert Bridge at St Budeaux West on 27 October 1975. It is about to cross the bow string bridge over the former LSWR main line, now the Gunnislake branch. 4M05 was always a busy train whatever the time of the year, and its load of 13 assorted vans shows up nicely from this angle. From the fifth van, one can plot the course below of the LSWR route by the gentle curve of its lineside fence.

D1048 *Western Lady*

'The Lady' was a firm favourite with many, and was the first to appear in the BR Rail Blue livery with full yellow ends. The loco is in fine form at Burngullow on 13 September 1971, as it heads 1B65, the 10.30 Paddington–Penzance, past the impressive Blackpool clay works. The tall structures to the left were for the clay slurry, last loaded from here in 2007, while beyond these plumes of steam are emitted from the kilns that operated between 1955 and 1984. This once busy site finally closed in 2013 and is now waiting its fate for the location is to be turned into an eco-village.

'The Lady' would last until the type's final day in traffic when, with D1010, it shadowed the 'Western Tribute' farewell tour. Even when there were just five locos remaining in the final period of operation, they were often seen on 1B39, the 10.40 Paddington–Plymouth; just like this climbing the 1 in 46 gradient of Rattery Bank towards Tigley at Dorsley Park on 31 January 1977, in glorious winter sunshine. As far as I can ascertain, this was the penultimate occasion this train was Class 52 hauled.

D1049 *Western Monarch*

One of the not intended benefits of the then recently opened A38 Plympton bypass was that its passage over the railway provided a superb vantage point on the gentle curve at Tavistock Junction. With its signals and signal box along with the up marshalling yard behind the latter, it was still a busy place on 2 November 1971. This is where I captured D1049, which had emerged from Swindon Works five days previously, its glistening paintwork complemented by a well-turned-out rake of mostly Mk.2 stock forming 1B25, the 08.30 Paddington–Penzance.

Spring time in Cornwall with D1049 in a sylvan setting as it traverses the nine arches of Forder Viaduct, just to the west of Saltash, on 25 March 1974, with 1V76, the 09.20 Liverpool–Penzance. The local landmark of the tower of St Stephens-by-Saltash church can be seen creeping into the picture at the top left corner. The section from Wearde, where we saw D1019, to St Germans was not part of the original route, this being a substantial inland deviation opened in May 1908.

D1050 *Western Ruler*

If one was out for an afternoon's photography after the early shift, this was a useful train to capture. The 14.00 Exeter Riverside–Truro goods (7B33) is seen here with D1050 in charge on the curve approaching Tresulgan, between St Germans and Menheniot. The early summer flowers are showing up well on 29 May 1974.

By this time, the inroads of the Class 50s were increasing and the number of Westerns in traffic was correspondingly decreasing. However, the sight of a Class 52 in Cornwall in charge of the up 'Cornish Riviera' was still very much the normal scene. D1050 on 1A19, the 10.50 Penzance–Paddington, makes its first intermediate stop at St Erth on 8 June 1974; no doubt to pick up a fair contingent from the connecting train from St Ives. This is a scene that has changed little in the intervening years to now.

D1051 *Western Ambassador*

Moving on the five miles from St Erth to the end of the line, a brace of Westerns is captured in the morning sunshine at Penzance on 27 May 1974. To the left, D1030 is at the head of 1M85, the 07.40 to Liverpool Lime Street, while to the right and certainly not on a Class 8 train is D1051, waiting to follow with the 08.00 Bank Holiday Monday excursion to Paignton. Yes, the railway really did run special trains like this to the seaside and popular they were.

So to another Cornish terminus and one where the Westerns made a few brief appearances in their final year of life. On 29 August 1976, D1051 has arrived at Falmouth with 2B70, the 08.22 Truro–Falmouth, the stock having reached Truro the previous evening off the 18.27 from Paddington. The engine is about to propel the coaches to the run-round loop, the ensemble then reversing back to form the 09.10 to Paddington. This service was diagrammed for a Class 50 but being on the night shift at Plymouth with the right people likewise at Laira paid dividends!

D1052 *Western Viceroy*

Part of my duties as the Rest Day Relief Clerk at Plymouth included covering in the Telegraph Office, situated on the fourth floor of the tower block, which gave a grandstand view of the proceedings at the station, and I always had a camera with me. If it was a nice morning, work was often interrupted, as was the case, for example, on 27 March 1970, Good Friday, when D1052 arrived with a 5Z90 empty stock move from Penzance. To the far left of the picture, the tracks leading to Millbay were still in situ.

The Westerns were mixed traffic engines capable of handling anything that came their way. A prime example was in South Wales where it was not only the Swansea–Paddington expresses where the class held sway; they also saw much work on freight duties, especially with the then life-blood of the valleys, coal trains. Seen on 6 April 1974, D1052 heads east through Newport with 8A39, the 12.00 Radyr–Acton, conveying domestic coal to keep the capital warm. Sadly, trains like this are no more. To the right, a Class 08 stands in the once busy Godfrey Road Yard.

D1053 *Western Patriarch*

The bridge taking a footpath over the line in the shadow of Restormel Castle, near Lostwithiel, was an excellent location for photography in both directions, and one that I attended on a number of occasions; every time I went there in the hydraulic era, D1053 appeared. It's strange how fate plays its hand. A classic scene was recorded at Restormel on 8 May 1976, as D1053 passes by with a very smart looking 1B03, the 07.30 Paddington–Penzance. This view for trains heading west is still available but a large tree has in recent years put paid to anything going east.

The ascent of Dainton Bank; if only I could bring you the sound that was echoing around the countryside as D1053 passes the Stoneycombe Sidings signal box up distant signal and heads towards Dainton Tunnel with 1B65, the 13.30 Paddington–Penzance, on 28 April 1976. Do not believe the headcode as this is certainly not a London-bound train. It was around this time that the need to show headcodes had been dispensed with by the authorities, and shed staff had yet to come up with the idea of showing the engine number instead.

D1054 *Western Governor*

A picture not of the greatest technical or scenic merits, but one I consider very special as this was my first colour slide taken of a Western. A gleaming D1054 stands in Platform 7 at Plymouth on 11 June 1965, ready to take 1A84, the 14.30 Plymouth–Paddington, to the capital. By this stage, the era of steam was over in this part of the world and these new-fangled diesels would be with us forever, would they not? Little did I or anybody else realise at the time but, within a dozen years, they too would have been despatched to that big engine shed in the sky.

The loco was often referred to by many of the hydraulic-following fraternity as 'The Governor'. A classic location recalling the rich heritage of the mining era in west Cornwall, D1054 passes the iconic Hallenbeagle Engine House adjacent to the Wheal Busy foot level crossing, just to the east of Redruth, on 27 October 1973. The train is 1V72, the 07.06 Bradford Exchange to Penzance or down 'Cornishman', a working at the time that was almost guaranteed to be Western-hauled.

D1055 *Western Advocate*

West Cornwall again on the same glorious autumn day of 27 October 1973. Before moving on about 10 miles east to Wheal Busy for 1V72, D1055 was captured rounding the sharp curve at Gwinear Road working the 09.30 Paddington to Penzance (1B25). Note, to the right can be seen the remains of the Helston branch, which had survived for freight traffic until 4 October 1964. D1055 was instantly recognisable by a small yellow box on the driver's window ledge, this being the remains of an experimental windscreen wiper mechanism fitted in 1964.

Overleaf: Disturbing the peace and quiet of east Cornwall, D1055 glides onto Forder Viaduct in charge of 1A45, the 12.40 Penzance–Paddington, on the sunny spring day of 16 April 1974. To the top right, Trematon Castle keeps watch over the proceedings while, in the foreground, the tidal Mill Pond still has enough waters of the ebbing tide to reflect the houses and buildings of this part of the hamlet known as Antony Passage. Still waters and a Western, enjoy!

D1056 *Western Sultan*

One for the corner of a model railway with a fine display of semaphores as D1056 has just come round the curve to the right with 6A17, the 14.50 Penzance to Paddington milk and vans, displaying an incorrect headcode. It is the Falmouth branch that carries straight on, a reminder that the aim of the Cornwall Railway Company was to connect Plymouth with Falmouth. In the background is the embankment that carried the West Cornwall Railway to its own terminus at Newham, Truro, this still being in situ on 28 April 1970.

Fishguard Harbour is 261¼ miles and just as many light years from Paddington, and in the hydraulic era was one of the hardest places to reach as the rail link to the port only remained to fulfil connections with the Rosslare ferry. At this time of the year, 28 March 1972, there was just one daytime train to the Welsh coast, the 08.00 from Paddington, which was always a good bet for the correct haulage. D1056 has run round its stock off the 08.00 and is ready to return to civilisation with 1C08, the 14.00 to Swansea. Notably, the wooden GWR station nameboard was still in place.

D1057 *Western Chieftain*

The Easter Sunday diversions of 14 April 1974, are seen again, this time with D1057 leading 1A49, the 12.05 Penzance–Paddington, in unfamiliar territory as it speeds down Honiton Bank at Wilmington. The sheer folly of the singling of the former LSWR main line in June 1967 came to the fore on this day as the diverted trains took their place amongst an amended service from Waterloo, with some inevitable waiting around at the few crossing points existing at the time. This view of the single line is now very different today with substantial tree growth.

On more familiar territory, D1057 sweeps through Slough on its way to the capital on 17 March 1975, with 1V38, the 12.25 Birmingham New Street–Paddington, this displaying another incorrect headcode. Behind the train is the substantial goods shed with the industry of Slough Estates further back while, to the left, the short branch to Windsor & Eaton Central curves away. With the electrification of the line and other alterations to the infrastructure, it is a much changed shot from here now.

D1058 *Western Nobleman*

In those pre mobile phone days, you did not always know what was coming and even at this late stage in the career of the class, the railway could still come up with the odd surprise. I had come here to see D1013 on a Nottingham–Penzance railtour that it had taken over at Birmingham but, ahead of this, D1058 emerging from Parsons Tunnel was a complete surprise. This was on a Paddington to Plymouth football excursion for Fulham fans to cheer on their team at Home Park and was a welcome bonus in the glorious sunshine of 13 November 1976.

Moorswater is the most graceful of the Cornish viaducts and fittingly complements the outline of a Class 52. With the newly completed Liskeard bypass of the A38 road behind, D1058 crosses the valley of the East Looe River on the eight-arch, 147-feet maximum height Moorswater Viaduct with 1B11, the 08.30 Cardiff Central–Penzance, on 4 September 1976. Note also the masonry piers of the original Brunel wooden viaduct, which was replaced by its newer counterpart from 25 February 1881.

D1059 *Western Empire*

Staying very much in the same part of the world, just to the immediate west of Moorswater Viaduct, there is an occupation footbridge for access to the fields on the other side of the tracks, which remains in use today. The sheep seem blissfully unaware of the passage of D1059, which is heading west with 1V76, the 0910 Liverpool Lime Street– Penzance, on 4 May 1971. Other than some recently cut back vegetation, a pastoral scene can still be enjoyed here, although not with one of these as a daily sight.

Staying on the subject of Cornish viaducts, one of the lesser known and rarely photographed is Blackwater Viaduct where we see D1059 taking the gentle curve over the seven-arch structure, which has a maximum height of 68 feet. The Western is on the approach to the former Chacewater station with the down 'Cornish Riviera', the 11.30 Paddington to Penzance (1B45), on 27 October 1973. The 'B' in the four-character headcode for Cornish-bound trains had changed from a 'C' in May 1971 to denote these were to or within the Bristol Division of the Western Region.

D1060 *Western Dominion*

One of the early withdrawals from service and another camera-shy Western, D1060 is enjoying the sun, the sea and perhaps the sangria as it disturbs the tranquillity of the holidaymakers and day-trippers while hauling the 03.14 Stoke Etruria–St Blazey freight (6V53) on the approach to Spray Point. Captured on 23 July 1969, this was a gloriously hot summer afternoon on the Teignmouth sea wall. It was not unusual for the down china clay empties to call in at Exeter Riverside Yard and pick up additional traffic for Cornwall, this accounting for the rather lengthy train.

It is a dull afternoon as D1060 rolls into Bath Spa on 1C67, the 15.00 Paddington–Swansea, the train being formed of a neat rake of Mk.2 stock, other than the Mk.1 Full Brake and the two catering vehicles. This service was booked non-stop from Paddington to Newport (Bristol Parkway would not open until the following year) but, for some unknown reason on 15 October 1971, it had been diverted from the direct Badminton route to run via Bath and round the curve at Dr Day's Bridge, which would have added at least 20 minutes to the journey time.

D1061 *Western Envoy*

This was my last Western that needed 'copping' and since it spent most of its life working off Landore Depot, it had eluded me for a long time, even turning up in Plymouth on one occasion when I had gone over to South Wales in pursuit of it! I was serving a lengthy queue in the Enquiry & Reservation Office on 17 October 1970, when a colleague informed me that D1061 was standing in Platform 3 at the head of 1C30, the 08.30 Paddington–Penzance. On the pretext of having to go behind for something, the queue just had to wait!

The autumn colours hold sway on the edge of Dartmoor as D1061 accelerates away from Ivybridge Viaduct, which is just visible behind the tree to the far left of the picture, at Stowford while working 1A85, the 08.05 Penzance–Paddington, on 9 November 1971. At this point, the up direction lineside fence of the railway marks the boundary of the national park, the line entering the latter about a mile east of here and exiting from it when leaving Marley Tunnel.

D1062 *Western Courier*

It is a wet morning as D1062 calls at St Austell with 1E21, the 10.25 Penzance to Bradford Exchange 'Cornishman'. To the right and still in use on this date, 11 May 1974, is the goods yard, which also at this time doubled as the Motorail terminus. On the opposite platform note the blue BRUTE (remember them?), or British Railways Universal Trolley Equipment, introduced in 1964, which were a common sight all over the system until they were phased out upon the demise of the Red Star parcels service in 1999, another reminder of how our railways have changed.

Very familiar to many these days as one of the seven examples of the class to be preserved, when in BR service D1062 was not all that keen on filling the lens of my camera and when it did, it tended to do so with a noticeable absence of any sunshine. However, I did catch it on the fine morning of 23 April 1974, storming out of Platform 4 at Plymouth at the head of 1M85, the 07.40 Penzance–Liverpool Lime Street, and passing the former North Road East signal box, which was demolished in March 2003.

D1063 *Western Monitor*

Early one morning at Paddington as D1063, displaying the headcode 1A60 off its previous working, the 19.15 Milford Haven–Paddington passenger and mail, brings in a rake of empty stock from Old Oak Common to form the 08.00 to Fishguard Harbour, this going forward with D1027. Behind the train is the splendid GWR 1930s architecture of the Westbourne Bridge office block, which still stands proudly today. At this time, 10 July 1970, it housed the British Railways Board offices and stores for records.

Overleaf: One of those special moments that stay in the memory forever and a case of being in the right place at the right time. So it came to pass early one autumn afternoon as the mists were just clearing at Adopters Lock on the Kennet & Avon canal, just to the west of Crofton, that D1056 was heading west away from the camera with a 7B26 goods train as D1063 came the other way in charge of 1A69, the 08.35 Penzance–Paddington. A perfect setting for the two to exchange greetings on 26 October 1973.

D1064 *Western Regent*

A morning out with D1064 on the Birmingham's (1): Bleary eyed after staying awake most of the night after listening to D1040 most of the way from Plymouth on 1A49, the 22.10 from Penzance sleeping cars, D1064 was a welcome sight in Platform 3 at Paddington on 7 February 1975, coupled to the front of the 06.45 to Birmingham New Street (1M10), the station still being eerily quiet before rush hour. The driver had overlooked the correct letter in the headcode box, while the notebook tells me this was a one-minute time exposure at F11.

A morning out with D1064 on the Birmingham's (2): D1064 was taken all the way to Birmingham New Street arriving at 09.36, then the 09.55 DMU to Lapworth was used to capture, as above, D1064 on 1V68, the 10.25 Birmingham New Street–Paddington. After photographing D1040 going the other way on 1M11, I made my way to Didcot to pick up D1009 hauling 1C63, the 13.15 Paddington–Cardiff Central, and then D1030 on the 1A51 16.15 return service to Bristol Parkway. The day ended with D1057 from Taunton on the down 'Golden Hind'; a trip to dream of now.

D1065 *Western Consort*

Summer Saturdays are recalled as D1065 rounds the curve into Bugle with the 14-coach 10.05 Newquay to Newcastle (1E22) on 4 September 1976, the engine being instantly recognisable due to its then deplorable external state. To its immediate left is the Carbis Wharf branch, which closed in November 1989, while to the extreme left is the remains of the short East Wheal Rose mineral line that closed on 29 November 1964. It is now a completely changed view here with all traces of the mineral lines long gone while the Newquay trains are barely visible through an avenue of trees.

D1065 is photographed making light work of Rattery Bank near to the summit and is about to pass under an awkwardly sited and narrow bridge on the A385 South Brent to Totnes road, near to Culver Lane. On this day in March 1973, the loco was in charge of 1B45, the 11.30 Paddington to Penzance 'Cornish Riviera', while its external condition was much better than when photographed three years later in the above view at Bugle, This was no great surprise though, it having spent half of the previous year, from February to August 1972, in Swindon Works.

D1066 *Western Prefect*

A busy scene as D1066 passes the goods yard at Drump Lane, just to the east of Redruth station, on 11 May 1974, with the lengthy 16.40 St Erth to Acton milk tanks (6A21), the train crew having made a slight error putting in the headcode; perhaps they had their own in Cornwall! Sadly, this is very much a scene of the past as there is no evidence that Drump Lane Yard with its fine goods shed or the signal box opposite ever existed, while the viewpoint itself is no longer available as the footbridge is now caged in, preventing any photography.

D1065 hurries along on the through line at Tiverton Junction with 1A19, the 11.00 Penzance–Paddington, on 1 August 1972, this view being taken from the signal box. The station closed on 12 May 1986, when it was replaced by the new Tiverton Parkway station, located two miles to the east. The signal box lasted until 21 March 1987, when the Exeter Panel took over, while the station buildings were demolished in April 1991. The overgrown and inaccessible platforms remain today as well as both the strategic up and down loops.

D1067 *Western Druid*

A scene that typifies the ethos of the Western Region in the hydraulic era as D1067 approaches Dawlish Warren in glorious winter sunshine on 12 December 1970, with 1C55, the 12.30 Paddington–Penzance. The engine fits in nicely between an array of lower quadrant signals, which are complemented by the wooden sign informing passengers that they are not allowed to cross the railway except by the bridge. It was a timely appearance by the loco as just nine days later, the Druids would gather at Stonehenge for the winter solstice.

Looking resplendent in maroon livery in the late afternoon spring sunshine, D1067 makes the St Austell call with 1M78, the 17.45 Penzance–Manchester Piccadilly, on 11 May 1968, complete with an ex Southern Railway parcels van next to the engine. The shot was taken during a break on the 'Clayliner' railtour, which was enjoyed in single car DMU W55016, this traversing many mineral lines that are no longer with us, much like D1067. For a change, it is nice to be able to report that this view has barely changed.

D1068 *Western Reliance*

The yacht in the foreground will soon be literally high and dry due to the ebbing tide as D1068 passes over the causeway at Golant with the afternoon clay empties, running as the 15.40 Carne Point, Fowey to St Blazey. Not all of the clay hood wagons actually have their hoods up, but the train is of neat appearance and fits in well with the surrounding Cornish countryside. Seen on 6 October 1976, the repaint of the loco from June 1974 has weathered a bit. Fortunately, the sight of clay trains going past this location can still be enjoyed.

Looking absolutely resplendent, having been released from the paint shop at Laira earlier that same day, D1068 has taken over the heavily loaded 12-coach 10.56 Paddington to Penzance (1B39) from Plymouth, and is seen here crossing Hayle Viaduct. One can only compliment the depot staff on their fine work. The train is slowing for the St Erth stop, where no doubt a large contingent will alight to change for St Ives, on 8 June 1974. The car park behind the garage may look a tad untidy but there is a good selection of now vintage vehicles on display.

D1069 *Western Vanguard*

D1069 at Kingskerswell was not in charge of 1Z15 as displayed but 2B32, the 16.55 Paignton–Plymouth, which was a convenient way to get the stock to Plymouth for the Sunday return working to Paddington. Recorded on 3 August 1974, the rear of the train is still passing beneath the impressive Grade II-listed Rosehill Viaduct, this featuring limestone piers and eight arches. It was built by Brunel for the branch to what is now Torre station and was notable for two reasons. It was masonry and not timber, and it was constructed to carry a road as the coming of the railway here bisected the village.

Overleaf: It is a hazy summer's day in mid-Cornwall as D1069 hurries through the former Burngullow station, closed on 14 September 1931, with 1A75, the 14.35 Penzance–Paddington, on 29 July 1972. Curving into the right of the train is the still extant Parkandillack freight branch which, until 6 February 1966, was a through route to St Dennis Junction. The line westwards from here to Probus was singled in 1986, but due to the problems of congestion this caused, it was re-doubled in 2004. This view is now very overgrown with vegetation.

D1070 *Western Gauntlet*

While this is an obvious angle from the Tamar Road Bridge to photograph trains going into Cornwall, the best results are only possible for a month or so either side of the June solstice and on a late evening when the sun is still high in the sky and far enough around for the correct lighting. You need a suitable train with the correct motive power for this all to fall into place, just like when, at around 20.00 on 29 May 1974, D1070 observed the 15mph speed limit as it crossed the Royal Albert Bridge and headed into Cornwall.

A pleasant rural scene as D1070, working 1B53, the 12.26 Paddington–Penzance, descends the 1 in 70 grade from Burngullow at St Stephen's, near Trebullan, on 29 June 1972. The train has now left the china clay area behind; the white outline of the Blackpool clay works and its fumes are just visible to the top left of the picture. This is part of the main line singled between 1986 and 2004, and the view is now overgrown. However, a visit to this area is recommended as the nearby St Stephen's Bakery does one of the best pasties to be had in Cornwall.

D1071 *Western Renown*

D1071 eases slowly along the causeway at Rundles Walk, on the approach to St Blazey, with 1M95, the 08.45 Newquay–Manchester Piccadilly, on 21 August 1976. The water course in front of the train is the short canal from St Blazey to Ponts Mill that opened in 1835. This was replaced by a horse-worked tramway built alongside it on its banks, which became part of the Newquay branch we know today in 1874. To the left of the causeway is the bubbling River Par, while Prideaux Woods on the hill behind makes for a nice backdrop.

A couple of weeks on from the above view and in the same part of the world, it is only about 2½ miles from St Blazey to the summit of the main line between Par and Lostwithiel at Treverrin. The beautifully backlit milk train has just emerged from the 565-yard Treverrin Tunnel as D1071 with 6A21, the 16.40 St Erth–Acton, begins the descent down to Lostwithiel on 7 September 1976. The signal behind the train was the first colour light example to be installed on the Cornish main line in 1956, it replacing the signal box here.

D1072 *Western Glory*

The glory of the hydraulic era. It is high tide as D1072 eases its way onto the 11-arch St Germans Viaduct, also known as Tiddy Viaduct, with a lengthy 14.00 Exeter Riverside–Truro goods (7B33), this being the view from St Germans Quay on 7 March 1974. The train is 106 feet over the waters of the short River Tiddy, a tributary of the River Lynher, which itself is a feeder of the River Tamar. This is one of the younger viaducts on the Cornish main line and opened on 19 May 1908, when the inland deviation from Wearde, near Saltash, was opened.

Same engine, same train, different location, different load; D1072 is seen passing Harford, near Ivybridge, and is once again in charge of the 14.00 Exeter Riverside–Truro. This was when the railway was still a major carrier of freight and the range of traffic carried varied from train to train and day to day. Of particular interest behind the loco on 28 February 1975, are the two carflats conveying an impressive selection of vehicles of the day. I am informed by Steve Andrews that the leading vehicles are a Morris Marina, Austin Mini, Austin Allegro and a Rover P6.

D1073 *Western Bulwark*

Getting to grips with the climb out of Plymouth station, D1073 is roaring those Maybach engines as it passes the Royal Eye Infirmary with 1A79, the 14.40 Penzance–Paddington, on 3 June 1974. The points, track and ballast are all very shiny as there had been a major track layout and signalling alteration scheme at the station from 10 March to 5 May that year, which had involved the engine sidings seen here. It has all yet to get that weathered in look.

Western water! After a night of heavy storms and torrential rain, I am riding right up behind D1073 as it literally makes waves on 1C16, the 08.10 Bristol Temple Meads–Plymouth, on 10 July 1968. With permanent way staff in attendance, the train is proceeding at 5mph through the flood waters over the level crossing at Hele and Bradnich, and then through the former station. Nowadays, such disruption would cause panic with line closures, diversions via Honiton if that was still open, and the dreaded rail replacement buses if any could be found.

Western Soliloquy

This book was written as an ENTERPRISE to a much loved class of locomotive, which when they were introduced were very much a PATHFINDER, EXPLORER and PIONEER in the field of main-line diesels. Amongst the titans of the track, they had that unique spirit of being a CRUSADER and a VENTURER which would take them far and wide, and would indeed prove their qualities as a real STALWART and be the TALISMAN for others to follow.

They flew like a HARRIER. In some parts they were regarded as an INVADER but there was one who spread their word as a valiant CAMPAIGNER for the cause. On the move, we recall the noise of an engine best described as a THUNDERER and the thrill only a real FIREBRAND can deliver.

Over the system they proved to be a far-reaching RANGER, a truly awesome LEVIATHAN of speed and a CHAMPION of all things hydraulic. They fought adversity as a true GLADIATOR, very much proven as a worthy WARRIOR, a brave BUCCANEER and one to be a CHALLENGER. All this made them very much a respected HERO of the rails. Maybe at times they were a bit CAVALIER, but to watch over them and keep check they had their own SENTINEL.

Were they military in style? FUSILIER battled to the very end. Many like me on the lineside became a HUNTSMAN in pursuit of that army of brave names and traditions such as GUARDSMAN, CENTURION and the record-breaking LANCER. Maybe we also thought of them as honourable soldiers, a true HUSSAR and a LEGIONNAIRE of honour. How we admired the firepower of MUSKETEER, RIFLEMAN and a crack MARKSMAN. Each was a faithful TROOPER to the cause, a DRAGOON of the highest order, and surely in the world of diesel locomotives a YEOMAN that stood out.

The once green EMPEROR and his EMPRESS brought to mind that the class were indeed SOVEREIGN as KING and QUEEN of the metals that stretched west from Paddington to the more distant parts of Cornwall and Wales. In this domain were to be found further members of royalty: a PRINCE with the beauty of a PRINCESS, the dignity one would expect of a DUKE, the grace of a DUCHESS, a VISCOUNT of elegance and the manners of a MARQUIS. They had their own LORD of all they surveyed and a LADY of quality who became a firm favourite with many devotees of the class.

Thus it was we gave them due respect as a MONARCH with the dignity of a great RULER. Many saw them on their travels as a true AMBASSADOR of the Swindon tradition, a VICEROY who could perhaps also be a PATRIARCH for the cause, and in times of trouble a GOVERNOR to keep order.

Their word was surely spread by that great ADVOCATE who led the way of those who represented high office from distant parts, SULTAN brought thoughts of the Far East, CHIEFTAN perhaps had a Scottish influence, and both surely were true NOBLEMAN of this great hydraulic EMPIRE. It was a DOMINION held together as heralds such as ENVOY travelled the system and their message was carried daily by a COURIER. All were kept in check by a MONITOR who if required would make way for a REGENT who had his own CONSORT for company.

Order was kept by a PREFECT. Days of distant past were recalled by a DRUID whose RELIANCE came to be a VANGUARD for any who would throw down the GAUNTLET.

It is with much RENOWN we remember the GLORY days of the Westerns, an era whose BULWARK we will never see the likes of again, one fondly entrenched in the hearts of many.